WICKED WILLIE'S GUIDE TO WOMEN

The Further Adventures of MAN'S BEST FRIEND

WICKED WILLIE'S GUIDE TO WOMEN

The Further Adventures of MAN'S BEST FRIEND

Cartoons and captions by Gray Jolliffe

Text by Peter Mayle

Harmony Books
New York

THE ETERNAL TRIANGLE, REVISED VERSION

At the risk of causing dismay to novelists, play-wrights, poets and writers of soap operas and soulful movies, we must point out a basic flaw in one of the world's favourite dramatic devices.

The eternal triangle – one woman torn between two men, or one man torn between two women – is bunk. It has only enjoyed such a long run because delicate artistic sensibilities tend to shudder at the truth. Shakespeare (whose first name, significantly, was Willie) came close to putting his finger on it when he had Lady Macbeth say, 'Is this a dagger which I see before me?'; but by and large the great story-tellers have been guilty of misleading us all. Either that, or they can't count.

A dagger? Who, moi?

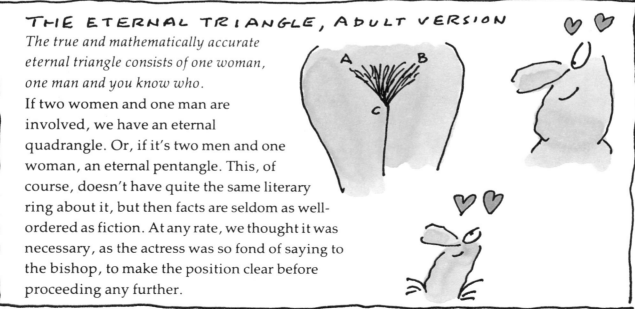

THE ETERNAL TRIANGLE, ADULT VERSION

The true and mathematically accurate eternal triangle consists of one woman, one man and you know who.

If two women and one man are involved, we have an eternal quadrangle. Or, if it's two men and one woman, an eternal pentangle. This, of course, doesn't have quite the same literary ring about it, but then facts are seldom as well-ordered as fiction. At any rate, we thought it was necessary, as the actress was so fond of saying to the bishop, to make the position clear before proceeding any further.

THE ONE-WOMAN SYNDROME: FREUD'S BIG MISTAKE

Invaluable though his contribution has been in the analysis of man's libido and the development of more comfortable consulting couches, Sigmund Freud's work can be criticized for one important omission: he never quite grasped the essential woman. Or if he did, he had his face slapped and gave up. Or maybe it was just that his couch could only accommodate one patient at a time. Whatever the reason, he failed to spot the fact that there are several distinct and very different female personality types.

This is evident from his endless muttering about 'the female of the species', as if there were just one all-purpose model. We now know, of course, that there are at least a dozen types – each type with its own whims and fancies, its own attitudes towards men and, perhaps most revealing of all, its own views on Wicked Willie's place in the scheme of things.

We can hardly blame Freud for taking the easy way out. The motivations that influence the female psyche are so complex that women themselves sometimes get bewildered, so it's no surprise that the male half of the population makes such a mess of it. One only has to look at the viewing figures for televised snooker to see that most men have abandoned the struggle to comprehend women in favour of watching something they can understand.

Women, on the other hand, have less trouble understanding men, as the following extract from psychiatric history shows.

MRS FREUD'S SLIP

Martha Freud never received the recognition she deserved, least of all from her husband, who was always too busy rummaging around in people's repressions to appreciate the virtues of his bride.

She was a businesslike woman, and it struck her one day that the Freudian couch was a sadly under-used asset; it was only occupied during office hours. Surely, she thought, in the interests of efficiency it would be sensible to take advantage of that free couch time. And anyway, why should Sigmund have all the fun?

So she began her own series of consultations, at off-peak rates, for the ladies of Vienna. Before long, she had amassed a body of highly unflattering research on the subject of women's attitudes to men. Not just the usual complaints about table manners or wearing the same pair of socks beyond the limits of social endurance, but disturbing comments of an intimate nature. And by far the most popular topic of consultation, as you might have guessed, was the little *Wiener Schnitzel* himself. In case after case, the same opinions emerged: he only thinks of one thing; he *wants* to be seen as a sex object; he never gets headaches; he can't hold his liquor; he is impossible to house-train; he disgraces himself in front of your best friend, and sometimes *with* your best friend.

Mrs Freud was thrilled with her findings. Sigmund wasn't, and sulked for several years. But it is thanks to her fearless research that we can now identify and describe woman as she really is. Or, since the types sometimes merge rather confusingly, woman as she really are.

THE FUNDAMENTAL DIFFERENCE BETWEEN WOMEN AND MEN

BASIC WOMEN

This can never be a definitive collection. Society is changing every day; we have already seen the first woman astronaut, the first woman jockey, the first woman's football team and the first woman judge. It is only a matter of time before we see the first convicted female mugger, the first woman president of the Old Etonian's Association, and the first female Hamlet. These changes will inevitably have their effect on the feminine persona and add to our basic list.

Note: Men studying this section will recognize at least five types. Women will recognize their dearest enemies. Hairdressers will recognize everybody.

THE SENSIBLE WOMAN:

THE FEMALE PREDATOR:

THE OTHER WOMAN:

THE GIRL WHO CAN'T SAY NO:

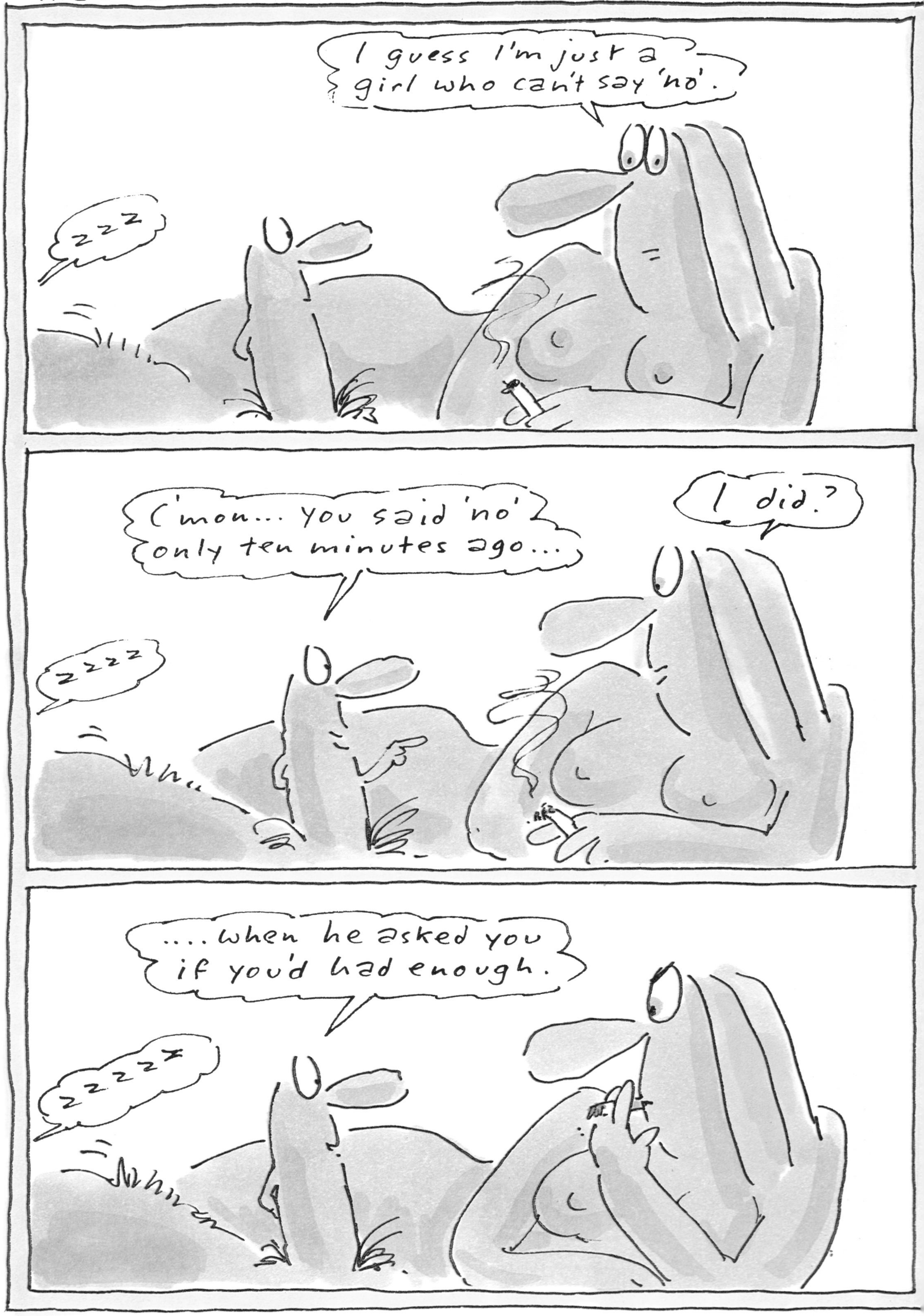

THE 'ALTERNATIVE' WOMAN:

THE INTELLECTUAL:

Have you read Marx on Socialism and the Proletariat?

No, but I've red marks on my willie...!

Sorry — but I'm afraid you've lost me...

Sending the port the wrong way has be subject of many cartoons and jokes, and in the da. when people cared seriously about the conventions, was a shocking social gaffe. Periodically there is a query and a new set of theories as to why the port goes round from right to left, clockwise. Theories have included the course of the earth around the sun, the bad luck and black magic associated with things going anti-clockwise, the primitive belief that only the right hand should be used for good important actions, and I have even heard

The only inevitability is that there will be fie. competition – and a great deal of that will be for the funds and finances of private investors. As the public become more and more interested in investing ir shares, and as the professionals lower their com mission rates and begin to deal in lower sums of money to attract the man in the street, so the whole market will be opened up to private investors. By October, many more private investors will be buying and selling shares (and consequently becom concerned about their whole range of fina

Right!

There's only one thing for it..

..Plan B.

THE SCHOOLGIRL:

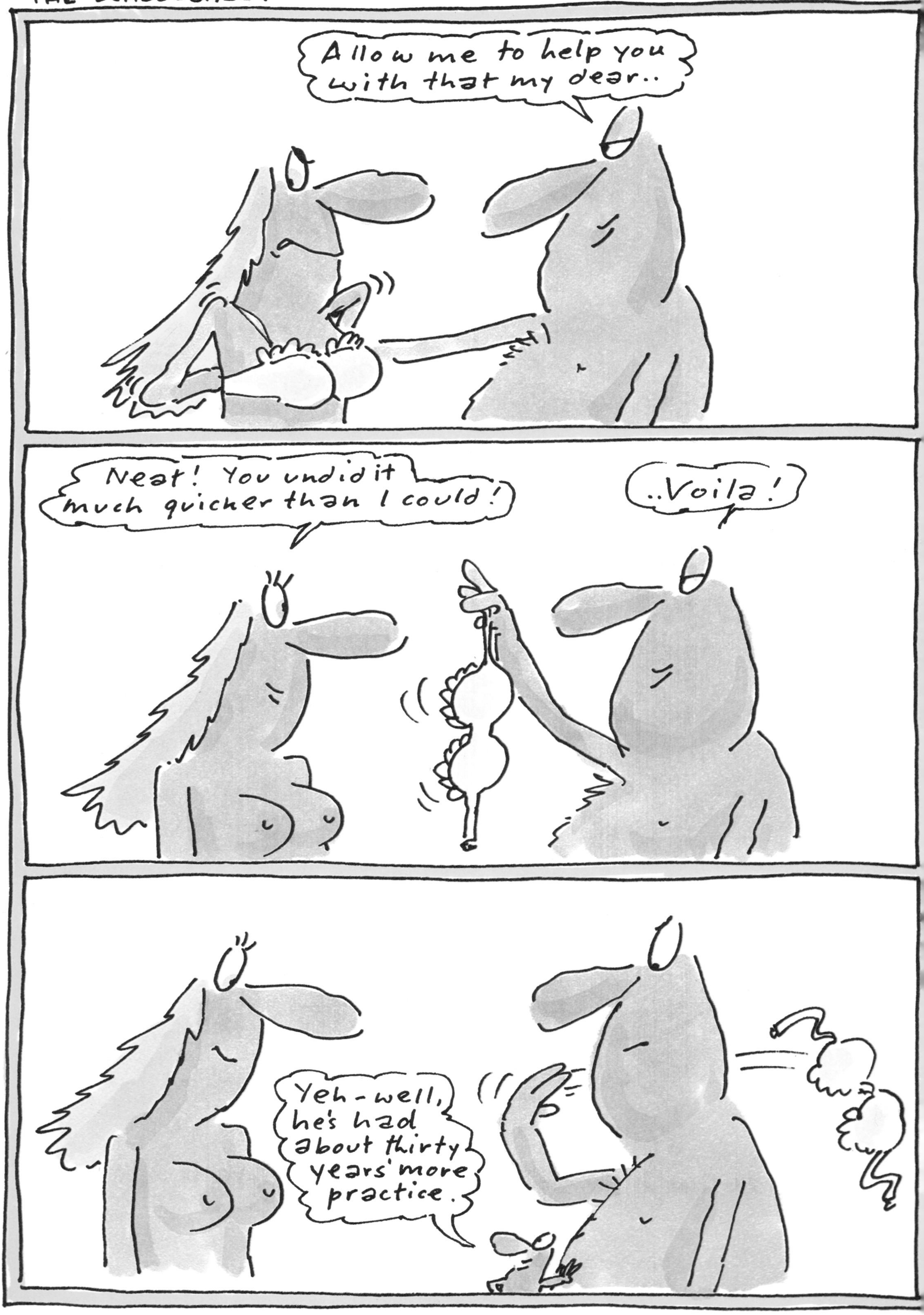

ONE OF THE BOYS:

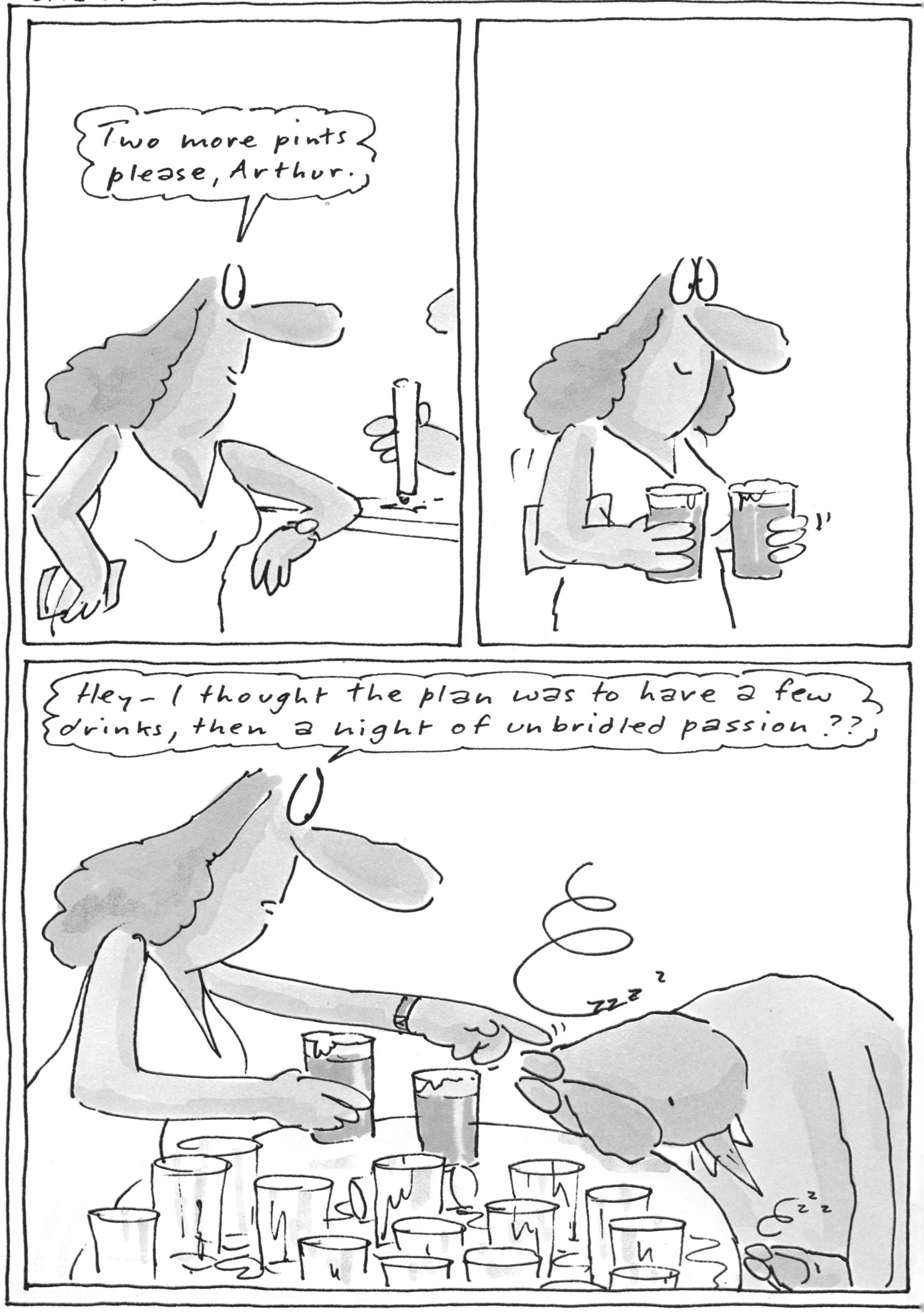

THE UPWARDLY MOBILE PRINCESS:

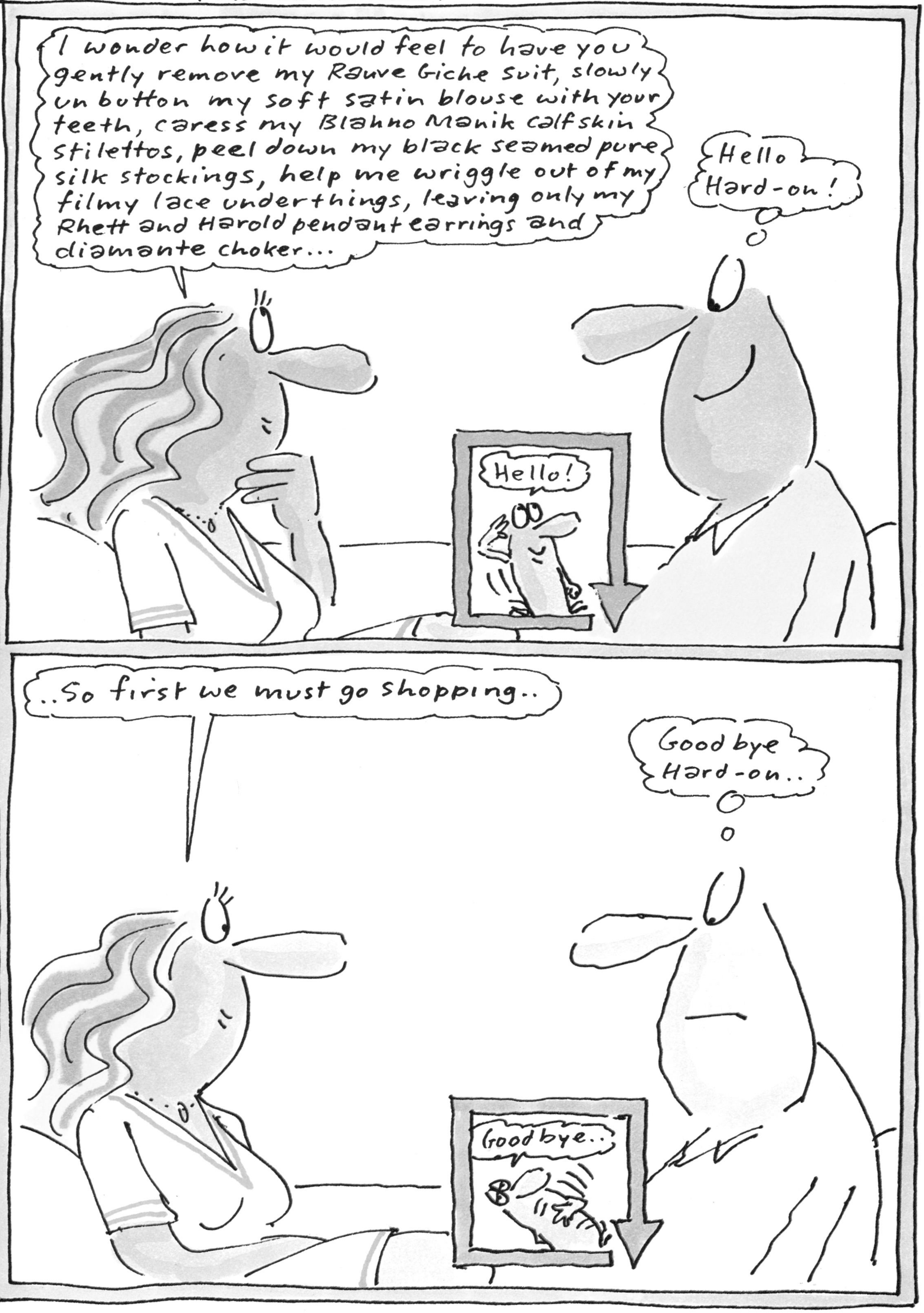

THE DIVORCEE:

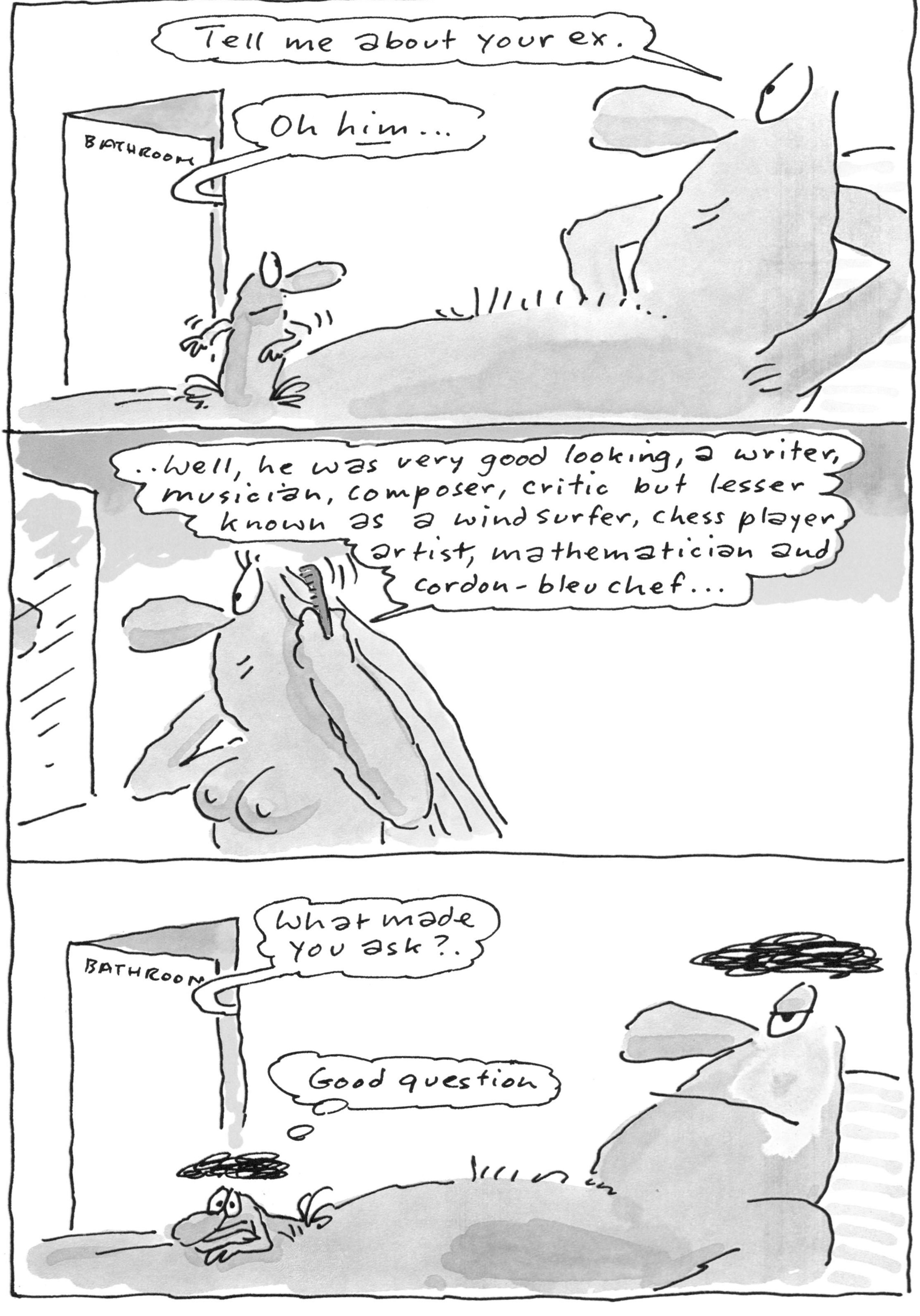

THE MILITANT:

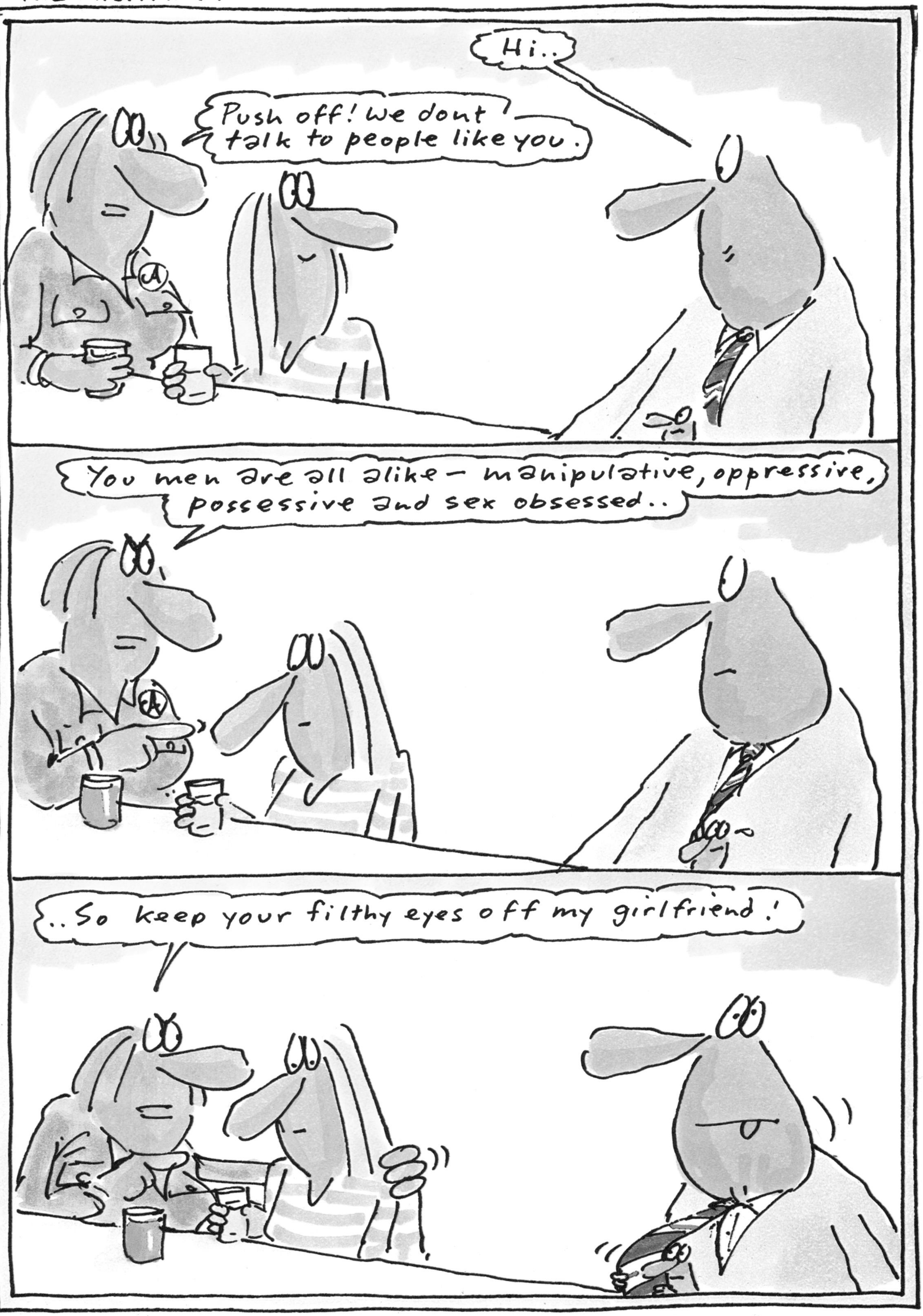

THE TEASE:

THE CAREER GIRL:

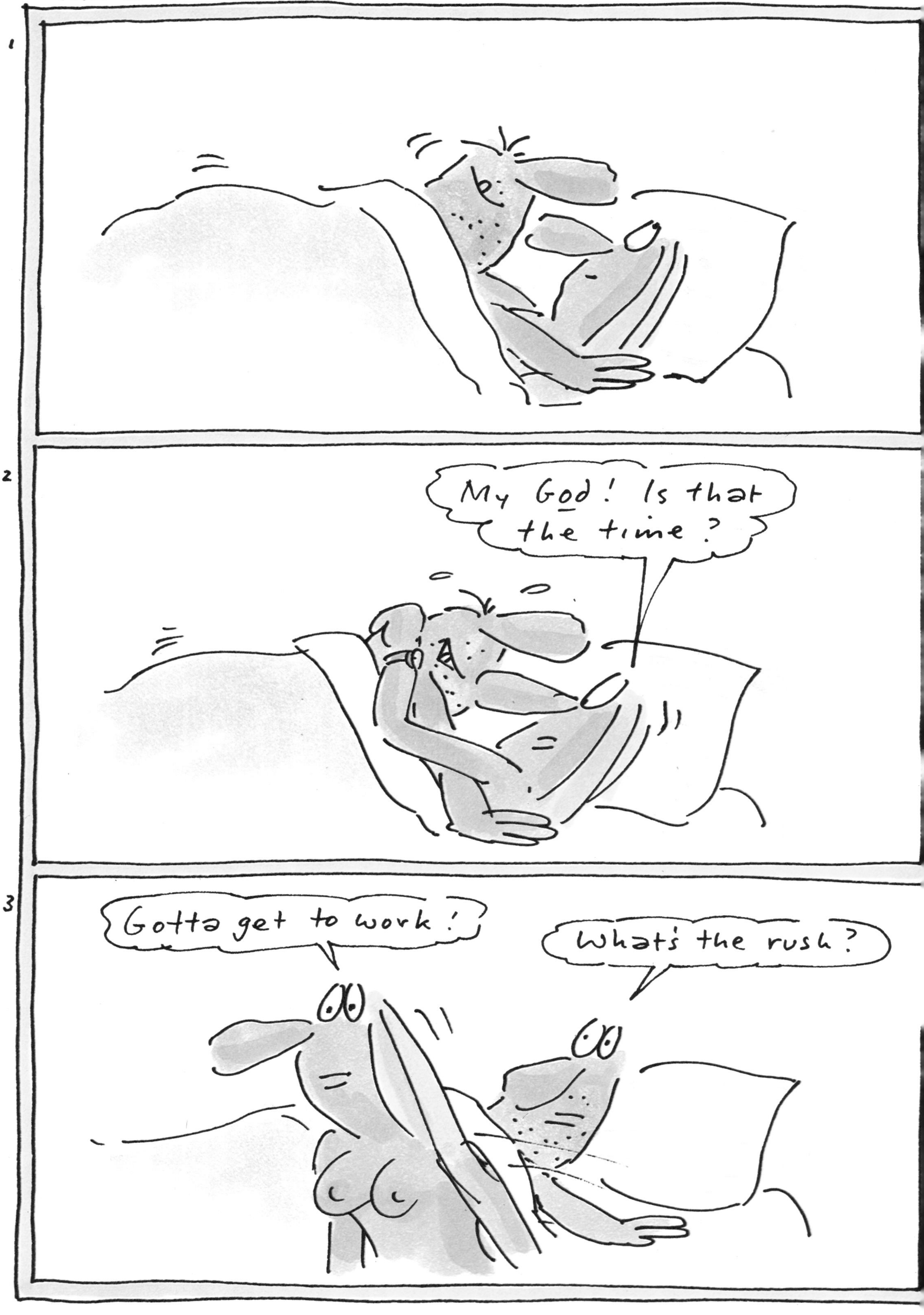

THE COMEDIENNE:

THE RELIGIOUS GIRL:

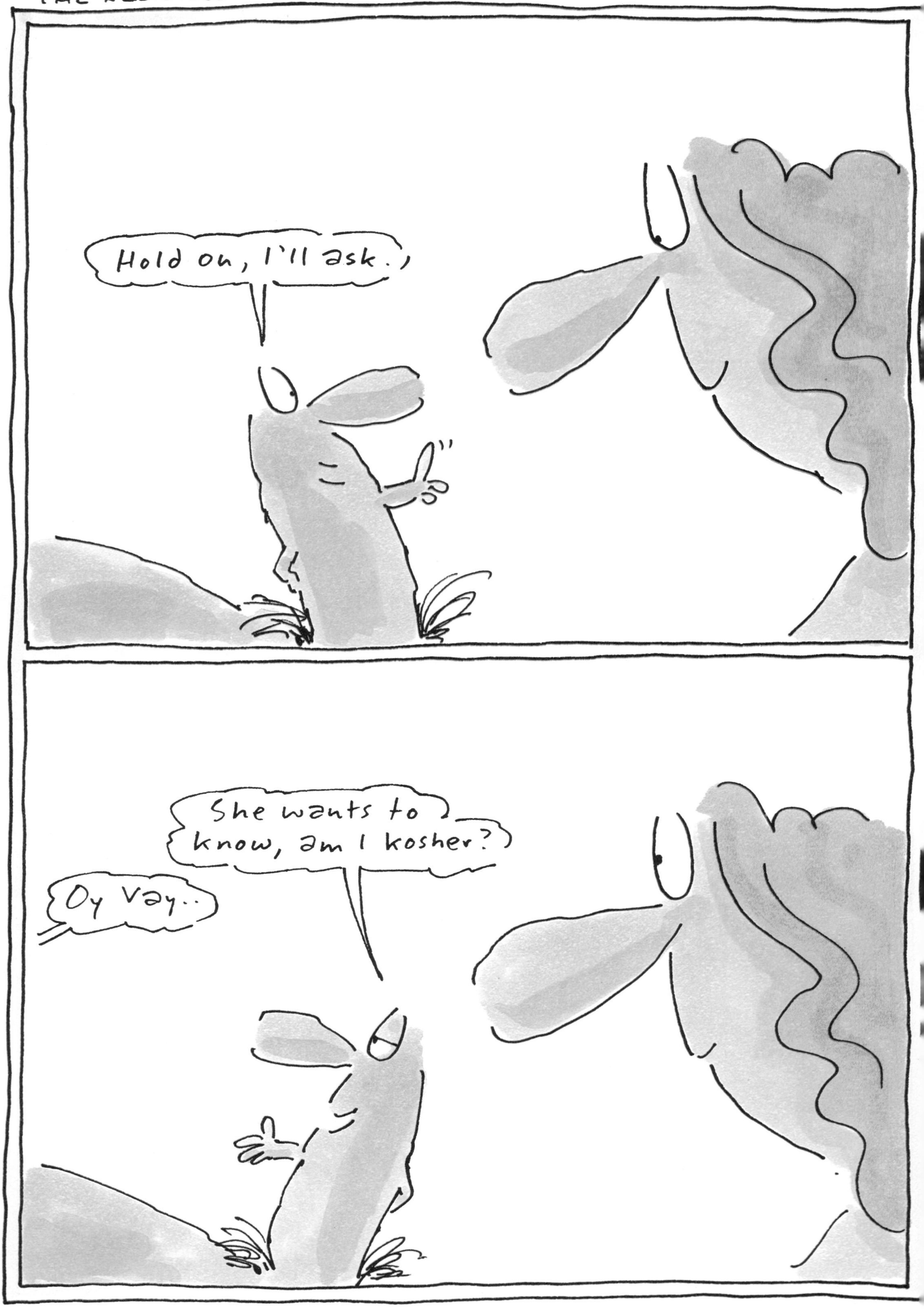

THE COMPULSIVE LIAR:

THE WOMAN BEHIND EVERY GREAT MAN:

THE WOMAN ON TOP OF EVERY GREAT MAN:

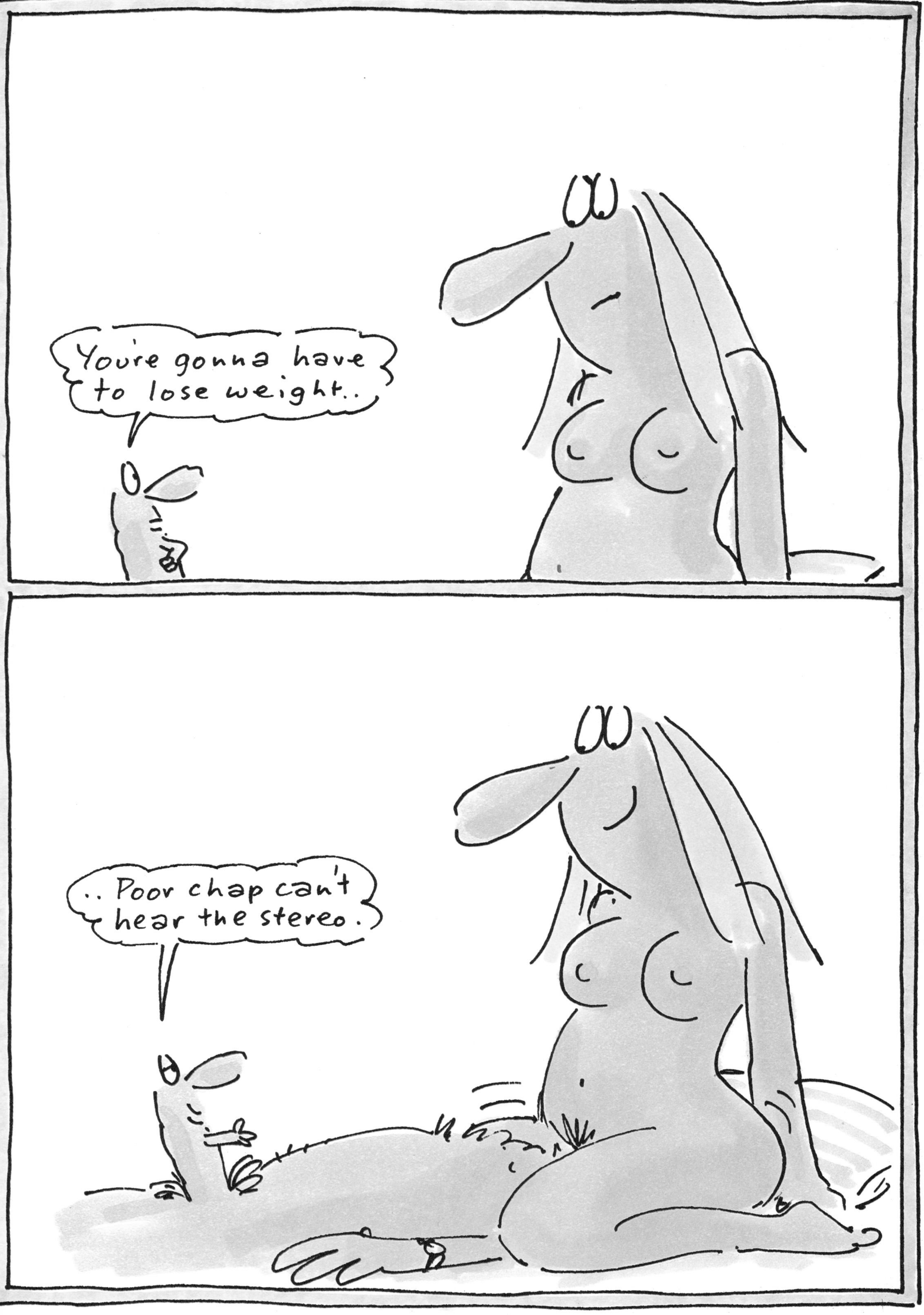

MORE TROUBLE

As if dealing with women on a private and personal level weren't difficult enough, there is a further set of pitfalls awaiting us whenever we venture into polite society. Failure to understand them can lead to tears, arguments, physical violence, breach of promise suits and persistent migraine.

The cause of the problem is very simple. A woman meeting a man socially will assume, very reasonably, that she is dealing with a rational and courteous being who is interested in what she has to say. A stimulating exchange of views, some light-hearted banter, a discussion about the Common Market or the true colour of Ronald Reagan's hair – in other words, a little pleasant social intercourse.

What the woman has failed to take into account is the third member of the conversation, whose interests are rather more limited. Sooner or later, his influence makes itself felt, and that's when the trouble starts. Indeed, we can see how widespread this influence has been just by looking at some aspects of contemporary life. Most of us accept them as perfectly normal and innocent. How wrong we are.

Why women visit the ladies in pairs

In any public place, but particularly in restaurants, even the most casual observer will notice that women hardly ever make a solo dash to the ladies' room. It seems to have replaced Noah's Ark as a destination that is best reached two by two.

This has been happening for so long now that it has become a minor tradition. In fact, there is a theory that it is the relic of an earlier tradition, going back to the days when the ladies withdrew after dinner to let the gentlemen savage the port and nuts and tell dirty jokes. Other students of sociology put it down to a wholesome desire for companionship while making running repairs to hair, makeup, laddered tights or gravy-stained jewellery.

Alas, there is a darker side to these expeditions. The reason women disappear in pairs is so that they can compare notes about what's been going on under the table. Bored by the conversation and only inches away from a female thigh, it is only a matter of time before something comes up that wasn't on the menu.

Believe me madam, I'd disown him if I could..

When all is revealed in the privacy of the ladies' room, the most common reactions are A) Outrage at being tampered with in between the breast of duck and the raspberry sorbet B) Disappointment at not being tampered with or C) The arousal of competitive instincts if both sides have been on the receiving end of Willie's attentions.

This explains why women can frequently go into the ladies' the best of friends and come out not speaking to each other.

Dare you to stand up.

Why men stand up when women enter a room

In the bad old days when men were men and women were horrified, civilized behaviour between the sexes didn't exist. Men were beasts. Women were pounced on and dragged into a convenient cave. Willie was in his element.

The feminine backlash, which started long before Boadicea and will go on long after Mrs Thatcher, is gradually taming the brutish side of man's nature. Nevertheless, vestiges of suspicion remain (quite rightly), and women still require some reassurance before they can feel at ease in mixed company.

The act of jumping to the feet has evolved as the most practical way of providing this reassurance. First of all because it is very difficult to pounce from a standing position. But more important, it also demonstrates that there are no immediate plans to unleash any concealed weapons.

Beware the man who remains seated. He obviously has something to hide.

Why men open doors for women

The sensible, brave and chivalrous arrangement for going through doors would logically be man first, woman second. That way the man would be the one to get it in the neck if there were anything dangerous or unpleasant waiting on the other side. So why, you might wonder, has the order been reversed?

A healthy instinct for self-preservation is the quick answer, but it would be wrong. To find the truth, we need look no further than downwards.

When you consider that most doors are made to admit one person at a time, you begin to see the attractions of what we might call a constricted social situation which offers the chance of illicit physical contact. There stands the woman in front of the closed door. The man, assuming he has placed himself correctly, has to lean across his companion to open the door. Unless he is cursed with supernaturally long arms, this brings the two bodies as close together as is possible without a complaint being lodged.

And that's not all. Under the guise of lending gentlemanly assistance (in case the woman is unable to negotiate an open door by herself), a helping hand is often applied to the area loosely defined as the lower back. A small but deliberate slip, and the helping hand finds itself on the upper slopes of the bottom. Now we know why women so often enter a room wearing a startled expression.

Why hand-kissing is almost extinct

It took women several centuries to realize exactly what was going on here. A kiss on the hand was generally seen as a mark of gallant respect. A good manicure job became essential. Lightly scented fingers clutching delicate scraps of lace handkerchief were offered, in the belief that the man was paying close attention to the charms of the female hand.

Unfortunately, the charms of the female hand had nothing to do with it. Nor did respect or gallantry. The ritual was merely an excuse for a brief but delightfully close encounter with the cleavage that presented itself at eye level as the man bent to kiss the offered hand. If it hadn't been for some men making pigs of themselves and going in for nosedives, we might still be a nation of hand-kissers today. (The French still are, but since the men are usually shorter than the women, *décolletage* remains safe from prying eyes.)

Why bar stools are the height they are

Nobody could accuse the inventor of the modern bar stool of designing a practical piece of furniture. Even for a sober occupant, it's uncomfortable. After a few drinks it becomes extremely dangerous, offering no lateral support and the prospect of a dizzy drop to anyone who is not fully in control of his equilibrium. It follows that there must be some non-functional reason for the high and precarious design.

There is. The sight of a woman in a tight and often short skirt arranging herself on a bar stool can bring tears to a strong man's eye and cause him to signal weakly for more champagne. Thus at a single stroke bar takings go up and the customer is kept happy. He is also likely to stay put, because to a connoisseur the only sight that can compare with a woman getting up on a bar stool is to watch her getting down while her skirt remains seated.

It's the same with car doors. Exit from a low-slung car is an impossible task for a woman to perform while keeping modesty intact. Ask any hotel doorman. He won't answer, but he'll smile.

It may seem as if Willie is having it all his own way in this category, but there are signs of female evasive action in the form of trousers. These have enjoyed a boom in the past 20 years, and we might have to take them seriously except for the fact that they are inherently ridiculous garments suitable only for people with hairy legs and unattractive knees – i.e. men.

BACK TO THE COUCH

For some unlucky men, this guide will have come too late. Baffled by the rich variety of women they have encountered, chastened and sometimes bankrupted as a result of mistaking one type for another, they will be licking their wounds and nursing their complexes over TV dinners for one.

Even Wicked Willie, resilient optimist though he is, may be disinclined to pick himself up and start all over again. We all have our little phobias and Willie, who hates to be left out of anything, has a few of his own. Some are physical, some emotional, but all of them should be taken seriously and treated with sympathy.

The first step in any successful course of treatment is to identify the nature of the complaint. Knowledge is supposed to cure all ills, and with this in mind we offer some comforting advice on coping with the after-effects of unsuitable liaisons – the painful souvenirs of life, love and the pursuit of the ideal woman.

For ease of reference, we can divide this section in two: *Deep Traumas*, where the cause of the problem is mental, and the more physically based *Fears and Loathings*. Wherever science has come up with a cure we shall mention it, but these are tricky and uncharted waters we're plunging into, and often the only immediate remedy is the one that Nietzsche used to prescribe: 'Take a couple of aspirins and come back and see me next week'.

The Napoleon Complex

The most common cause of this most common complaint is a peal of girlish laughter as you spring unclothed through the bedroom door. (It can also be brought on by a chance encounter with a prize marrow or a visit to an Italian delicatessen, in which case the condition is known as Salami Envy.)

In layman's terms, what we're discussing is a worry about lack of stature. Few things in life can dampen Willie's enthusiasm, but a feeling of inferiority is one of them, and it can have an instant effect on his bearing. He broods. He becomes shy and introverted, sometimes to the point of near invisibility, leaving you to make apologies for his lack of presence. It is not until a visit to the nearest museum and a detailed inspection of classical nude male statues that his spirits revive, as they invariably do when you realize that there's always someone worse off than you are.

I'd no idea you could talk..
Oh yes—but nobody ever listens.
Cigarette?
Why not?
Beer?
How kind!
Bed?
Blow in my beer and I'll follow you anywhere!
I'll just slip into something comfy..
So will I..
Aaaaarghh!
Not that emasculation nightmare again??
Don't worry! I'm still here!

The Oedipus Duplex

Usually found among younger men, this escalation of an old complex is brought about by recent advances in cosmetic surgery. In these days when major parts of the female anatomy can be lifted, tightened, tucked and generally adjusted, and when septuagenarians somehow

manage to retain the bloom of youth, it is alarmingly easy to leapfrog a generation. The mother fixation is taken an age further, and we find young men making whoopee with women old enough to be their grandmothers. To Willie, who can never see beyond the end of his nose, age is irrelevant; it's co-operation that counts. To his more thoughtful owner, however, there is the nagging fear that one day he might suffer the terminal humiliation of losing his lady love to a spry Old Age Pensioner.

Phantom Vasectomy

Another result of developments in surgical technique. Much has been written over the past few years (mainly by women journalists) about the benefits of vasectomy. It's quick, completely reliable, widely available and does away with all those bits and pieces that are always getting lost under the bed or swallowed by the cat. Who could possibly object to it?

Who else? Willie becomes very disturbed at the very mention of the word, seeing horrible visions of enforced early retirement caused by the doctor having hiccups at the crucial moment. In its advanced stage, this can develop from the standard Phantom Vasectomy into a form of creeping paranoia known as Fear of Scissors, inducing profound suspicion and regressive behaviour at the sight of everything from nail clippers to garden shears.

Doctors and Nurses

What used to be a harmless and amusing diversion has turned into a potential health hazard. Gone are the carefree games of Hunt the Thermometer. It's quite possible nowadays to find yourself playing Pass the Herpes without knowing it.

Willie's normal devil-may-care optimism is in conflict here with two other sides of his disreputable character. As a confirmed hypochondriac, he will imagine symptoms where none exist. And, vain creature that he is, the thought of picking up an ailment that might spoil his flawless complexion is enough to send him rushing to the bathroom mirror in panic.

In certain parts of America, it is apparently the fashion to exchange health certificates along with telephone numbers, and to meet for your first date in the doctor's waiting room. Who said romance was dead?

A LESSON FROM THE GREAT LOVERS

What is it that Casanova, Henry VIII, Lord Byron, Rudolph Valentino and one or two legendary milkmen have in common? A success rate with the ladies that, if fully documented, would put them all in the *Guinness Book of Records*.

It has often been said of these gentlemen that their hearts ruled their heads, but historians have shown a curious reluctance to tell us what it is that rules their hearts. Once again, the blame rightly belongs to the great optimist himself, who goes through life convinced that it never hurts to ask. More than that, he actually feels that women would be deeply offended if he didn't show a persistent interest in getting to know them *really* well. Shameless, energetic and determined to do the fair sex a favour, he makes the average door-to-door salesman look like a wallflower.

You can judge the effectiveness of this approach by merely looking around you. We all know at least one man who despite superficial disadvantages like lack of hair, lack of height, lack of money or lack of social graces still manages to cast a spell on a succession of personable and intelligent women. 'What', we wonder, 'can she possibly see in *him*?'

It's perseverance. As Casanova often found, the bedroom door might be locked but there's usually an open window somewhere. That's Willie's philosophy. Say what you like about him, but he doesn't give up without a struggle. And he knows that if the worst comes to the worst, it's only your face that's going to get slapped. He should worry.

THE LANGUAGE OF LOVE

The difference between what is spoken and what is actually meant has been an eternal source of confusion between man and woman. This has led to a certain amount of distrust between the sexes, to the point where a perfectly innocent comment, such as 'My wife doesn't really understand me', is enough to make most women reach for their excuses and head for home.

Who is to blame for these tragic breakdowns in communication? What is it that comes between two normal and well-adjusted adults to ruin a beautiful relationship?

If we don't know now we never will. It is, of course, the ever-present ulterior motive that lurks unseen (we hope) beneath the surface of seemingly respectable remarks. Here are some disturbing examples that illustrate the gulf which exists between the simple phrase as we hear it, and the conversation according to Willie:

WILLIE TRANSLATES:

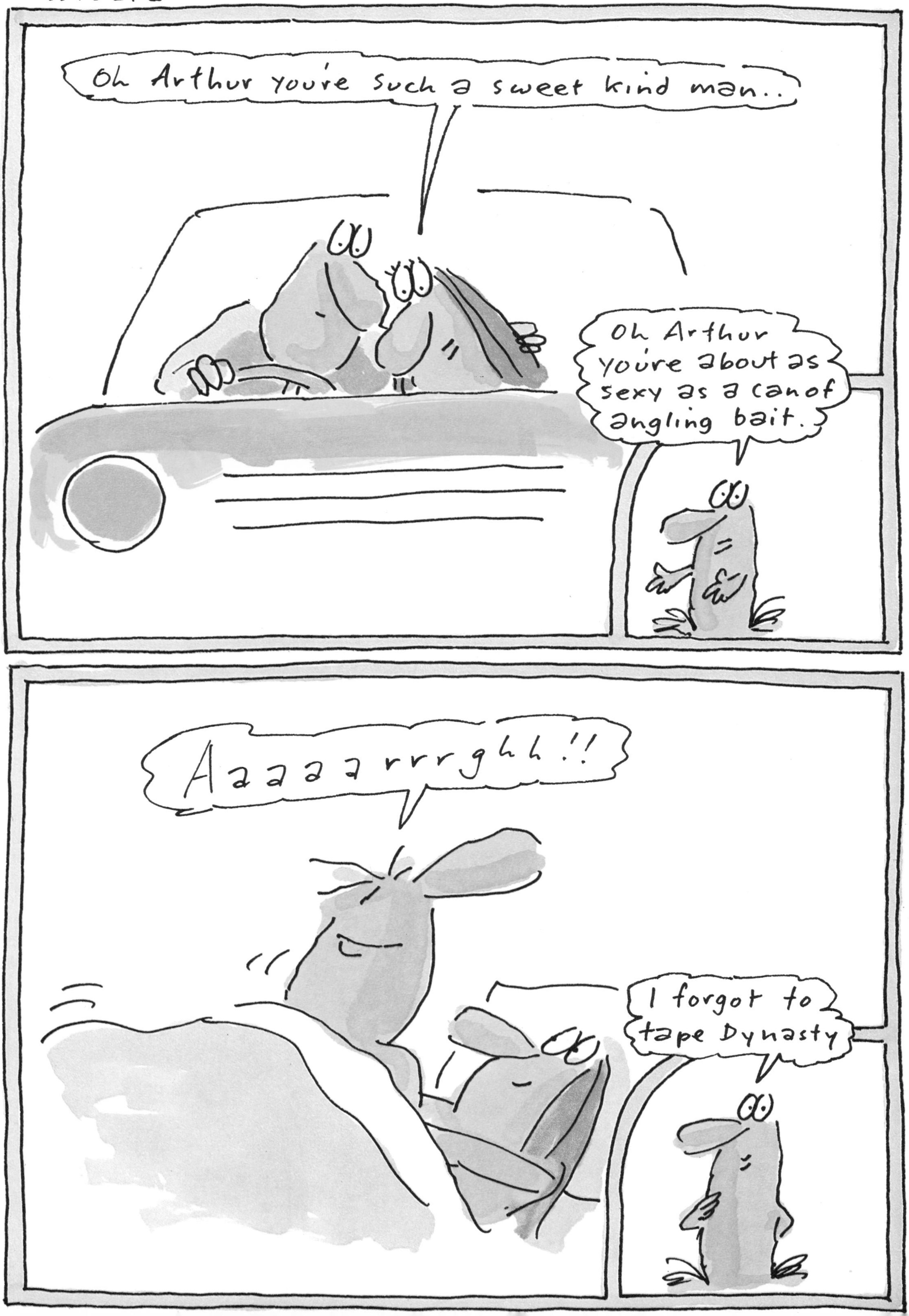

WILLIE TRANSLATES:

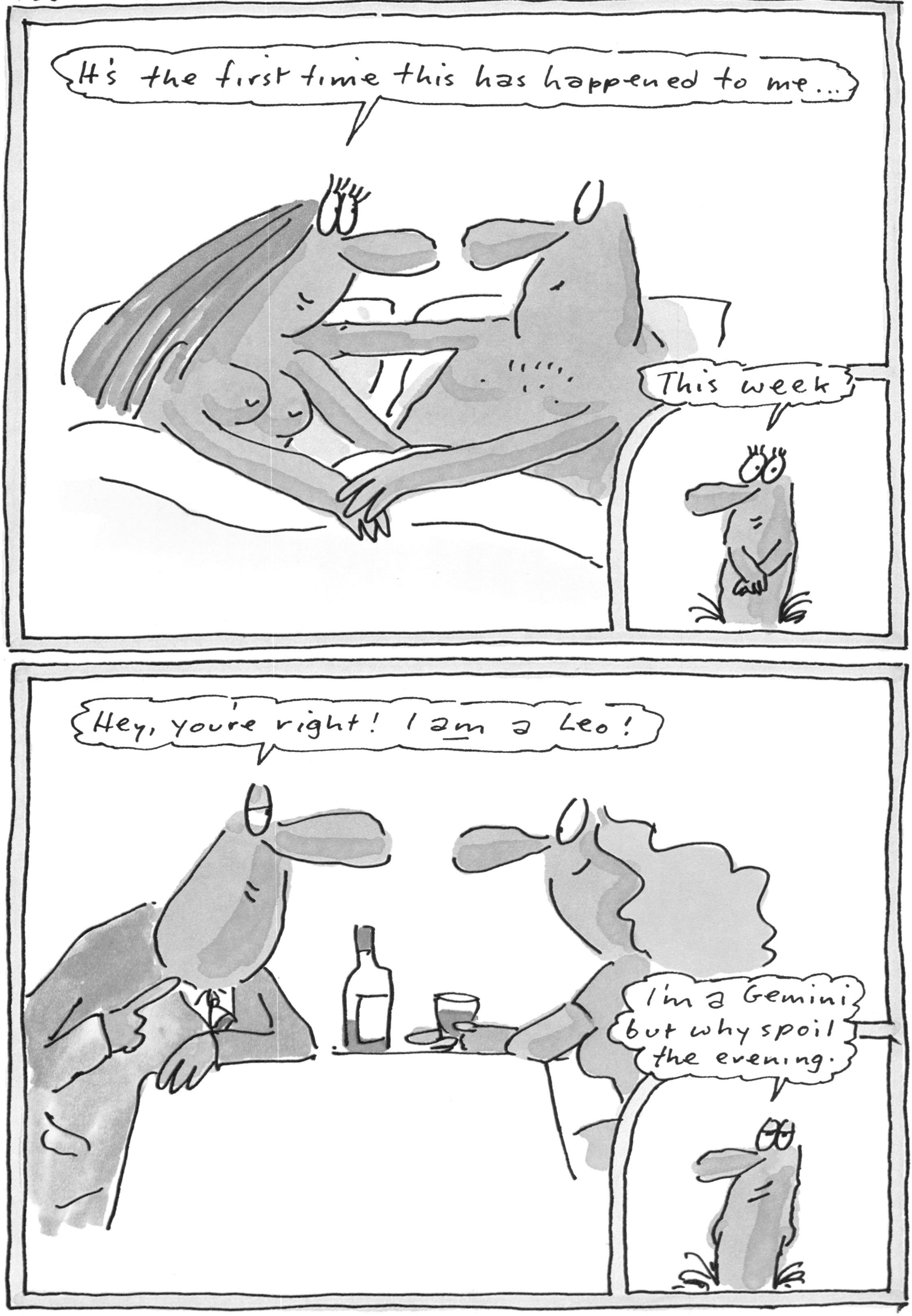

WILLIE TRANSLATES:

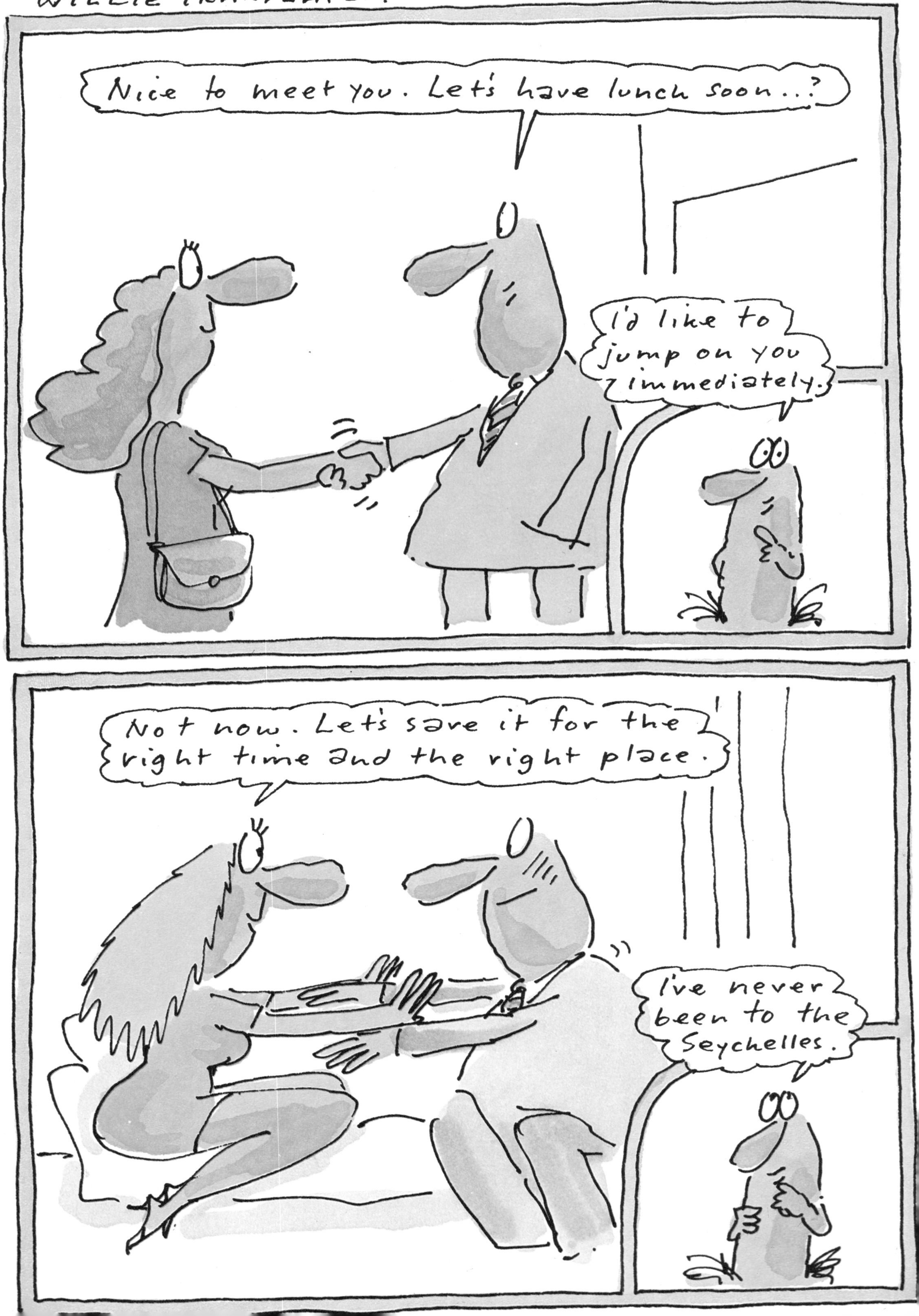

WILLIE TRANSLATES:

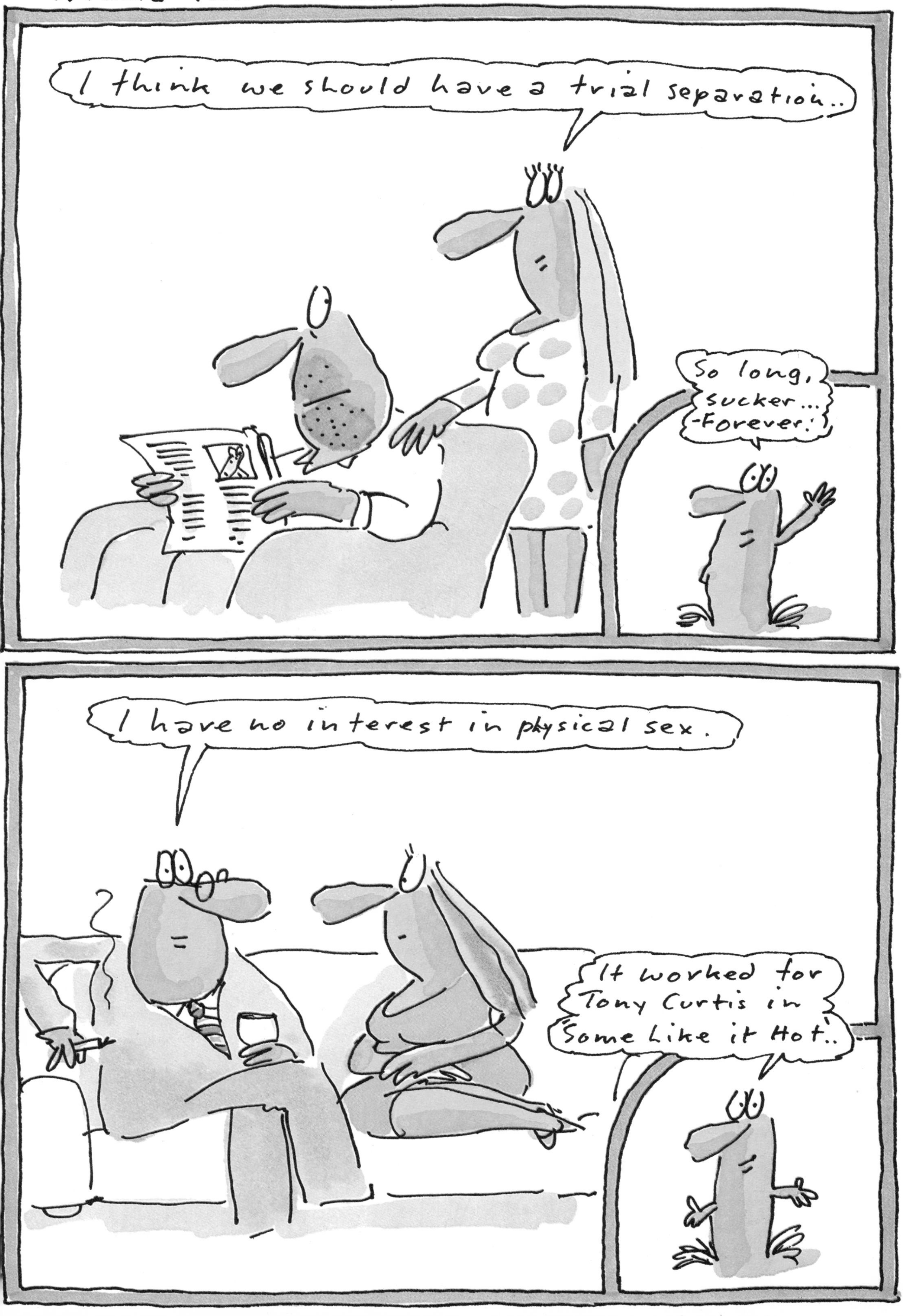

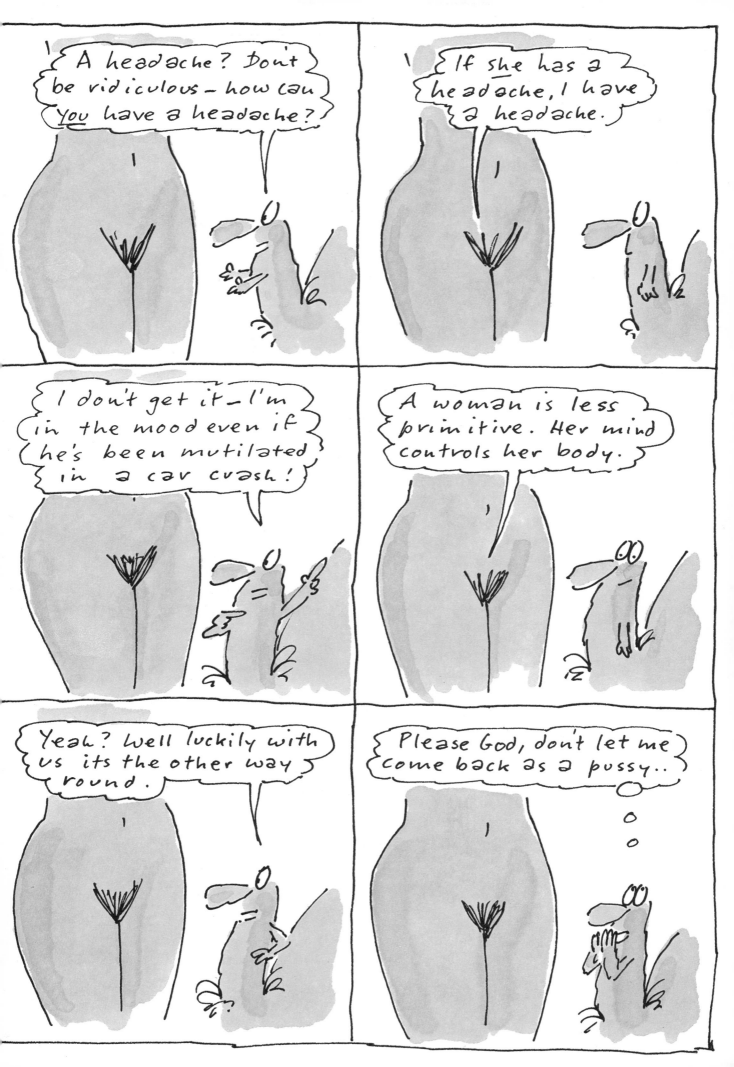

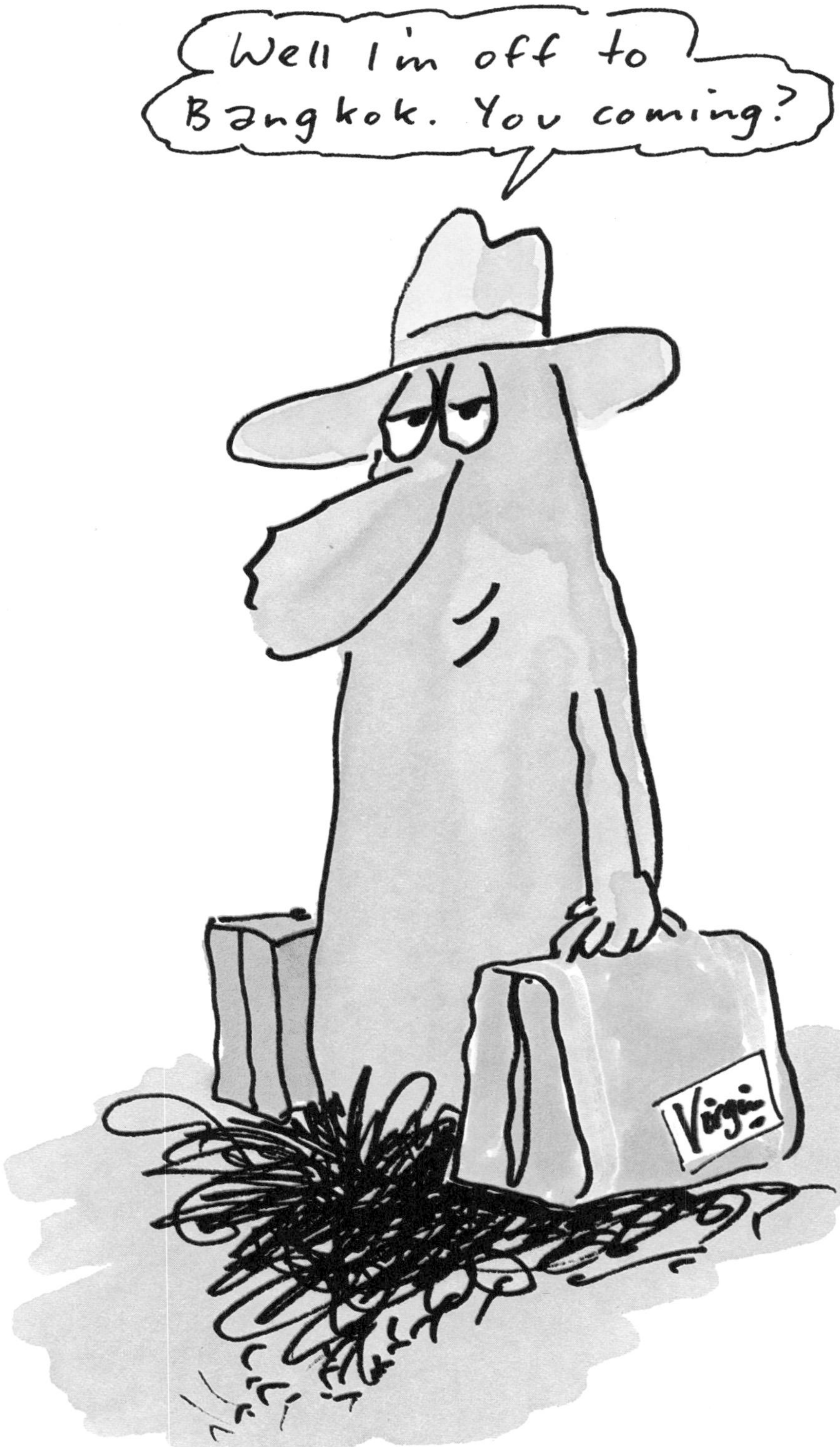
Well I'm off to Bangkok. You coming?
Virgin

Published in the United States in 1988 by Harmony Books, a division of
Crown Publishers, Inc., 225 Park Avenue South, New York, New York
10003, and represented in Canada by the Canadian MANDA Group

Originally published in Great Britain in 1986 by Pan Books Ltd.

HARMONY and colophon are trademarks of Crown Publishers, Inc.

Manufactured in the United States of America

Library of Congress Cataloging-in-Publication Data

Jolliffe, Gray.
    Wicked Willie's guide to women.

    1. Sex—Caricatures and cartoons. 2. English wit
and humor, Pictorial. I. Mayle, Peter. II. Title.
NC1479.J64A4 1987   741.5′942   87-18148
ISBN 0-517-56652-4

10 9 8 7 6 5 4 3 2 1

First American Edition